JB
McK

WILLIAM McKINLEY

OUR TWENTY-FIFTH PRESIDENT

by Cynthia Amoroso

THE CHILD'S WORLD®

Published in the United States of America

The Child's World®
1980 Lookout Drive • Mankato, MN 56003-1705
800-599-READ • www.childsworld.com

Acknowledgments
The Child's World®: Mary Berendes, Publishing Director

Creative Spark: Mary McGavic, Project Director; Melissa McDaniel, Editorial
Director; Deborah Goodsite, Photo Research

The Design Lab: Kathleen Petelinsek, Design; Gregory Lindholm, Page Production

Content Adviser: David R. Smith, Adjunct Assistant Professor of History,
University of Michigan–Ann Arbor

Photos
Cover and page 3: White House Historical Association (White House Collection)
(detail); White House Historical Association (White House Collection)

Interior: The Art Archive: 7, 13, 23, 31, 35 (Culver Pictures); Art Resource, NY:
22 (National Portrait Gallery, Smithsonian Institution), 30 (Snark); Associated
Press Images: 17 (White House Historical Association), 34 (The Hannah Lindahl
Children's Museum); The Bridgeman Art Library International: 37 (Private
Collection, Peter Newark American Pictures); Corbis: 9, 18, 28, 36 (Corbis), 24
(Bettmann); Getty Images: 29 (MPI); The Granger Collection, New York: 5 and
38, 20 and 39, 21, 27, 33 and 39; iStockphoto: 44 (Tim Fan); Jupiter Images:
11 (Stock Montage/Index Stock Imagery); Library of Congress: 19; McKinley
Memorial Library and Museum, Niles, Ohio: 8 and 38; The William McKinley
Presidential Library and Museum, Canton, Ohio: 4, 15, 16, 26; Ohio Historical
Society: 12 (Courtney Studio Collection); Rutherford B. Hayes Presidential Center,
Fremont, OH: 10; Stark County District Library, Canton, Ohio: 14; SuperStock:
25 (Culver Pictures); U.S. Air Force photo: 45.

Library of Congress Cataloging-in-Publication Data
Amoroso, Cynthia.
  William McKinley / by Cynthia Amoroso.
    p. cm. — (Presidents of the U.S.A.)
  Includes bibliographical references and index.
  ISBN 978–1–60253–053–9 (library bound : alk. paper)
  1. McKinley, William, 1843–1901—Juvenile literature. 2. Presidents—United
States—Biography—Juvenile literature. I. Title.

E711.6.A46 2008
973.8'8092—dc22
  [B]
                          2008002298

William McKinley served as president from 1897 to 1901.

TABLE OF CONTENTS

CHAPTER ONE

EARLY LIFE

When William McKinley became president in 1897, he was considered a model for other men. He was friendly and cared about others. He was careful not to embarrass himself, his family, or the people he represented. He worked long hours and put great energy into the things that were important to him. Today, he is remembered as a president with an excellent character who helped the United States become a world power.

William McKinley was born on January 29, 1843, in Niles, Ohio. His parents were William and Nancy McKinley. William Jr. was the seventh of nine children, although one of his siblings died in childhood. His father worked at a foundry, where iron was manufactured. Though McKinley worked hard to support the family, they did not have

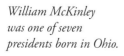

William McKinley was one of seven presidents born in Ohio.

much money. Still, William Jr. enjoyed a fun-filled childhood. He spent much time playing outdoors. He fished, hunted, swam, ice skated, and rode horses.

The McKinleys valued education. Even though he worked long hours, William Sr. always found time to read. He read the Bible and the plays of William Shakespeare. William's parents wanted their children to be well educated. As a young boy, the future president attended a one-room schoolhouse in Niles.

William McKinley was born in this house in Niles, Ohio, in 1843. At the time, making iron and steel were the town's major industries.

McKinley's parents were of Scottish and Irish descent.

Seven presidents were born in Ohio. Besides McKinley, they were Ulysses S. Grant, Rutherford B. Hayes, James A. Garfield, Benjamin Harrison, William Howard Taft, and Warren G. Harding.

In 1852, when William was nine years old, his family moved to Poland, Ohio. There he attended a private school called the Poland Academy, which was run by the Methodist church. Living in Poland was a sacrifice for William's father because he had to travel many miles back to his business in Niles. By this time, his hard work had paid off and he had become a partner in his own small iron-manufacturing company. He was away from home most of the time, returning home only on Sundays.

For this reason, William became close to his mother. She was responsible for raising the children and encouraging them to be successful in school. Nancy McKinley was very religious. It was important to her that William and his brothers and sisters follow the rules of the church. She taught them to work hard, to be respectful of others, and to be courteous and honest in everything they did.

William McKinley was a serious student who worked hard at his studies. He enjoyed reading, **debating,** and public speaking. He became the president of the Poland Academy's first debate club. Like his mother, he was deeply religious. With his strong religious beliefs and his talent for public speaking, William seemed to have the skills to be an outstanding minister. This idea made his mother happy. She always hoped that William would become a minister.

In 1860, when he was 17 years old, McKinley entered Allegheny College in Pennsylvania. After only a few months, he became very ill and was forced to

*McKinley worked as a teacher while he was still a teenager. He soon left his teaching job to fight in the **Civil War**.*

go home. McKinley planned to return to school as soon as he recovered from his illness. By the time he was well enough to go back, however, his family could not afford the cost of college. So in 1861, 18-year-old McKinley went to work as a teacher and as a clerk at the post office. He wanted to earn money so he could finish college. But events in the United States forced McKinley to delay his return to college even longer.

In the early 1860s, tensions in the United States were at the boiling point over the issue of slavery. Slavery was allowed in the Southern states but had been outlawed in the North. Some Northerners wanted to abolish, or end, slavery throughout the nation.

Two of McKinley's great-grandfathers fought in the American **Revolution**.

William McKinley joined the Union army in 1861. He served for four years.

The **Union** is another name for the United States. During the Civil War, the North was called the Union. The South was called the **Confederacy**.

Many more thought it should not be allowed in new **territories.** Most Southerners thought that new territories should be able to decide for themselves whether to allow slavery. They did not believe the national government had the power to say where slavery was legal. They thought those decisions should be left to the states and territories.

Southerners grew angrier and angrier. They feared that slavery would be abolished throughout the nation. Many of them thought they could never run their large farms, called plantations, without the free labor that enslaved people provided. They believed that ending slavery would end their whole way of life.

The arguments between the North and South eventually turned into violence. On April 12, 1861, fighting broke out between the North and the South at Fort Sumter in Charleston, South Carolina. This was the start of the Civil War.

McKinley's cousin, Will, was visiting him when they heard the news of the attack at Fort Sumter. Their loyalty to the Union and to the new president of the United States, Abraham Lincoln, was strong. They decided it was their duty to join the army. Both young men joined the 23rd Ohio Volunteer **Infantry.**

McKinley became a brave soldier. He entered every battle confident that he would not be injured. He was sure he would return home to his mother safe and well, just as he had promised her. The men in charge recognized McKinley's leadership skills and confidence, and

The Civil War began when Confederate forces began bombarding Fort Sumter on April 12, 1861. The Confederates won the battle, and Union troops surrendered the fort two days later.

During the Civil War, McKinley was given the rank of **brevet** major. After the war, he continued to be called "Major."

For a time during the war, McKinley worked delivering food to soldiers in battle. At the Battle of Antietam, he risked his life driving a wagon of hot food and coffee to Union soldiers on the front line.

he was given more responsibility. After especially brave acts, he was made an officer, a leader of other soldiers. He was proud to wear the bars on his uniform that indicated his position of leadership.

As an officer, McKinley served on the staff of Colonel Rutherford B. Hayes. McKinley learned many things from Hayes, who became McKinley's **mentor** and friend. This relationship continued throughout McKinley's life. Eventually, Hayes became president of the United States. This also influenced McKinley.

In April 1865, the South surrendered. The Civil War was over, and McKinley's service in the army was complete. When he returned home, he was a different man. He had a strong, muscular body and a **disciplined** character. He had also developed a strong interest in **politics,** the work of the government.

Like McKinley, Rutherford B. Hayes (right) was from Ohio. The two men became friends during the Civil War, and Hayes later helped McKinley win a seat in the U.S. House of Representatives.

A MAN OF STRONG CHARACTER

In a letter to his nephew James, William McKinley wrote about the importance of having a strong character. As James was entering the army in the late 1800s, McKinley wrote him, "I am deeply interested in your success and I want you to be a good soldier. Do everything the best you know how." Along with urging him to be a good soldier, McKinley offered James advice about his behavior. "Be careful about your writing. See that your words are spelled correctly. Better have a little pocket dictionary with you. It mars an official paper or letter to have a word misspelled." He also encouraged James to have a strong moral character. "Look after your diet and living. Keep your life and your speech both clean, and be brave."

CHAPTER TWO

POLITICAL LEADER

Now that his service in the army was over, McKinley had to make a decision about his future. He valued education and wanted to finish college. He was considering becoming a lawyer. He returned to Ohio in 1865 and began studying law with Judge Charles Glidden. About a year later, McKinley entered law school in Albany, New York. After finishing his law studies, he passed the necessary tests and became a lawyer in 1867.

At that time, his sister Anna was a principal at a school in Canton, Ohio. She wanted William to move there. After visiting her, he agreed that it would make a wonderful home. McKinley moved to Canton and worked with a local judge for a short time before opening his own law office. He won his first case as a lawyer and earned $25 for the work. At that time, $25 was a lot of money.

McKinley was a successful lawyer before entering politics.

McKinley quickly became an important member of the community. His deep faith and simple lifestyle made him fit in well in Canton. People were drawn to his thoughtfulness, his friendly laugh, and his pleasing personality. He made friends with many different kinds of people. He became the head of the Sunday school in the First Methodist Church and president of the YMCA. After only one year in Canton, McKinley had gained a reputation as an easygoing neighbor, an open-minded community leader, an able lawyer, and an excellent public speaker. In 1869, this

As a young man, McKinley led a very simple life. In fact, he had never tasted ice cream until he was a student in law school. The first time he tried the treat, he thought some custard had accidentally frozen!

The city of Canton was growing quickly at the time McKinley lived there. A large city hall was built in the 1880s (above).

popularity helped him get elected to his first public office, prosecuting attorney of Stark County. A prosecuting attorney is a lawyer who works with the police to make sure that people who break the law go to jail.

Another important event happened to McKinley in 1869. While doing business at a bank, McKinley met Ida Saxton, the daughter of the bank owner. Ida had fair skin, sky-blue eyes, and masses of reddish-brown hair. Many men were attracted to her, but she was not interested in them. Ida was well educated and came from a wealthy family. She had just returned from an eight-month trip to Europe. Although she was wealthy and popular, she was not satisfied with her life. At that time, women did not work in business. But Ida's father had other ideas. Ida began working in her father's bank to learn the skills of a businessperson.

When Ida saw William in the bank that day, she was immediately attracted to him. The two fell in love and were married in January 1871. Guests called the wedding and reception a "grand affair." After a honeymoon in New York, the McKinleys moved into a home on North Market Street in Canton. The home was a wedding gift to the couple from Ida's father.

Ida gave birth to their first daughter, Katherine, on Christmas Day in 1871. Six months later, Ida became pregnant with a second child. Just when the baby was to be born, Ida's mother died suddenly. Her death was hard on Ida, who was overwhelmed with sadness. She soon gave birth to the baby, a girl they named Ida. But baby Ida was unhealthy and died before she was five months old.

This was a very difficult time for Ida McKinley. Her health was poor. She developed a condition that made it difficult and painful to walk. She was very depressed and became

One story says that William McKinley and Ida Saxton had been walking together one day. When it came time to part, William said, "I don't like these partings. I think we ought not to part after this." Ida agreed, and the couple decided to marry.

Ida McKinley was wealthy and well educated.

15

terrified to let little Katherine out of her sight. Two years later, another tragedy occurred. Katherine got sick and died. After the death of her mother and two daughters, Ida became ill with **epilepsy.** This disease caused her to have attacks that sometimes made her faint. Sometimes she suffered violent **seizures.** Ida struggled with epilepsy and depression for the rest of her life. Her husband was devoted to taking care of her.

During this difficult time, McKinley continued to be successful in his work. He became increasingly interested in politics and decided to run for the House of Representatives, part of the U.S. Congress. With

When McKinley ran for the U.S. House of Representatives in 1876, he began wearing a scarlet carnation on the collar of his coat. From then on, he almost always wore a red flower. In 1904, the state of Ohio adopted the scarlet carnation as its official state flower in McKinley's honor.

McKinley was a handsome, friendly man who was popular with the people of his hometown. His personality helped him in politics.

Ida McKinley was sick for much of her adult life. William McKinley paid careful attention to her condition. He was always ready to help if she fainted or had a seizure.

this decision, McKinley left his law practice. He was elected to the House, moved with Ida to Washington, D.C., and began a long career in government.

One of his most important accomplishments was the McKinley Tariff of 1890, which helped protect American companies from foreign competition. A tariff is a tax on foreign goods, which makes **imported** products cost more. Tariffs encourage Americans to buy items made in the United States because they don't have the added tax. McKinley believed this would help not only the wealthy businessmen who owned American companies but also the workers who made the goods. The tariff made McKinley popular with Americans both rich and poor.

McKinley served seven terms in the U.S. House of Representatives. In Washington, he was known for being polite and patient. Other politicians remarked that he was the only man in Congress who had no enemies. Even so, he was defeated for reelection in 1891. He and Ida returned to Canton.

Later that year, McKinley made a political comeback. He was elected governor of Ohio and served from 1892 until 1895. As governor, McKinley proposed laws to protect railroad workers. He tried to find ways to stop child labor. At that time, many children worked long hours at difficult jobs. McKinley also supported laws to deal with problems between workers and large businesses.

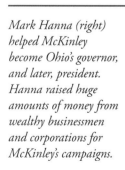

In 1896, the tallest mountain in North America was named for the future president. Mount McKinley sits in the middle of Alaska's Denali National Park. Although Mount McKinley is the peak's official name, most Alaskans call it Denali, its Native American name.

Mark Hanna (right) helped McKinley become Ohio's governor, and later, president. Hanna raised huge amounts of money from wealthy businessmen and corporations for McKinley's campaigns.

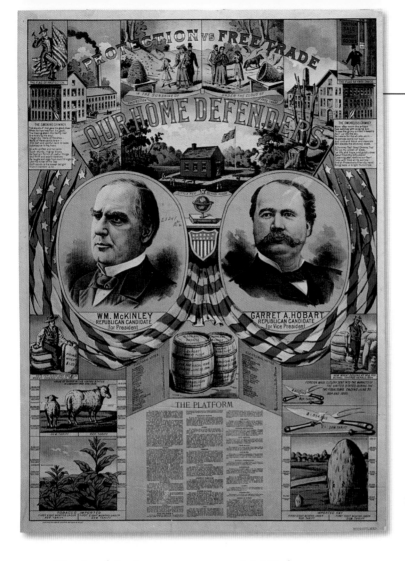

William McKinley ran for president on the promise of protecting American businesses. His vice-presidential candidate, Garret Hobart, worked as a lawyer for businesses and had little political experience.

During his time as governor, McKinley met a man named Mark Hanna. He was a powerful businessman who owned several mines. Hanna helped raise money for McKinley's political **campaigns.** In fact, he helped raise more than $3.5 million for McKinley's first presidential campaign. This was a record amount of money at the time. Hanna also became one of McKinley's most important advisers.

In 1896, the Republican Party chose McKinley as their **candidate** for the upcoming presidential election. The vice-presidential candidate was Garret

McKinley campaigned for the presidency from the front porch of his Canton home.

Hobart, and Mark Hanna managed the campaign. At this time in history, presidential candidates did most of their campaigning by riding trains across the United States. They stopped in towns and cities along the way to give speeches and meet people. McKinley's opponent, William Jennings Bryan, was an excellent speaker. People around the nation met Bryan's train to get a glimpse of him and hear him speak.

Because McKinley's wife needed his care, he would not leave her to campaign in this way. Instead, he held a "front-porch" campaign from his home. More than 750,000 people traveled to Canton to hear him give campaign speeches. Newspapers all across the United States printed his words. In addition, McKinley was the first candidate to hand out campaign buttons and other items to promote himself as a candidate. His campaign was successful, and he won the largest number of the people's votes since Ulysses S. Grant in 1872. McKinley was about to become the 25th president of the United States.

McKinley campaigned for the presidency from the front porch of his Canton, Ohio, home. Another president from Ohio, James Garfield, had been the first candidate to try a front-porch campaign. In 1881, Garfield became the 20th president. To carry on the tradition, Warren Harding also campaigned from his Ohio home. In 1921, Harding became the 29th president.

In 1893, the United States suffered the worst economic downturn in its history up to that point. During the 1896 presidential election, McKinley promised to bring the nation prosperity.

21

PRESIDENT MCKINLEY AT WORK

What does a president do during each day? McKinley had a busy schedule. He would usually have breakfast at about 9 o'clock each morning, read the newspaper, and be at his desk by 10 o'clock. He would then have meetings with other officials until he left at about 1:30 in the afternoon for lunch with his wife. He returned to his desk by about 2:30 and worked until 4:30.

Almost every day, he would take a carriage drive with Mrs. McKinley through the streets of Washington, D.C. Some days he would ride several miles on horseback or take walks near the White House. He would then return to his office to read telegrams and the evening newspaper. McKinley would have dinner at about 7 o'clock and always appeared at the dinner table nicely dressed. After attending social events, McKinley would return to his office and work until about midnight each night. McKinley attended church every Sunday. He never worked or attended public events on Sundays.

CHAPTER THREE

A WORLD POWER

During his campaign for president, McKinley expressed his concern for the people of the United States. As president, he wanted to change laws and do things that would help the American people and make their lives better. What he didn't expect was how much time he, as president, would have to spend on problems that concerned the people of other countries rather than Americans.

At this time, many Americans were convinced that the United States needed to be a world power. But the United States was not very involved with other countries. The nation didn't import or **export** as many goods as it does today. But more and more people believed that the United States should take a greater interest in the world. They were worried about how people in other

William McKinley in 1899

The warship USS Maine exploded in the harbor in Havana, Cuba, in 1898. No one knows what caused the explosion, but newspaper owners such as William Randolph Hearst blamed Spain. Newspaper headlines were worded in ways that made Americans even angrier with Spain.

countries were being treated. They were worried about how the behavior of governments in other countries might affect the United States. But not all Americans agreed that the United States should interfere with other countries.

When McKinley began his presidency, many Americans were concerned about Cuba, an island in the Caribbean Sea about 90 miles (145 km) south of the tip of Florida. Cuba was fighting for its independence from Spain. Many politicians wanted the United States to help Cuba. Even many newspapers became involved in the issue and encouraged the president to take action. McKinley felt pressured by public opinion.

As president, McKinley hoped to focus on problems at home. Unfortunately, problems with other countries took up most of his time.

In January 1898, he sent the battleship USS *Maine* to Havana, Cuba, to protect American interests there. McKinley also tried to get Spain to **negotiate** with Cuba on the issue of independence. Then, on February 15, 1898, the USS *Maine* mysteriously exploded while in the Havana harbor. More than 270 of the ship's 354 crewmembers were killed in the explosion. There was no way of knowing whether Spain was involved in this incident. But many Americans believed Spain was behind the explosion and wanted the United States to declare war.

McKinley knew that a war with Spain was likely, but he attempted to resolve the conflict in other ways. He sent messages to Spain demanding an end to the conflict in Cuba. He also demanded that Cuba be given its independence. McKinley searched for ways

After the USS *Maine* sank, many Americans called for an attack on Spain. The phrase "Remember the Maine" was used by people who wanted the United States to attack Spain.

McKinley's **inauguration** was held at the Capitol on March 4, 1897.

At first, McKinley did not want to become involved in the trouble between Cuba and Spain. But once the United States declared war on Spain, McKinley was dedicated to victory. He is shown here (seated at center) meeting with a general and his staff.

During his presidency, McKinley often spent his evenings playing cards, answering letters, and taking walks or carriage rides.

to peacefully end the conflict. He said, "War should never be entered upon until every agency of peace has failed." McKinley's attempts to negotiate a peaceful solution failed. On April 25, 1898, the U.S. Congress declared war on Spain.

The Spanish-American War involved battles on the island of Cuba and on the seas surrounding it. Because Spain also had colonies in the Philippines and other islands in the Pacific Ocean, the United States sent ships and troops to those areas as well. The war lasted only about 100 days before the United States won. The most important battle took place in Cuba. Theodore "Teddy" Roosevelt and a group of soldiers called the Rough Riders fought at San Juan Hill. During the battle, U.S. ships formed a **blockade** in the Santiago Harbor and trapped the Spanish fleet of ships. Roosevelt then led his Rough Riders up San Juan Hill and took possession of the area. The Spanish-American War ended shortly after this battle.

In August 1898, the United States and Spain signed an agreement to end the war. This agreement became known as the **Treaty** of Paris. After it was signed, the United States took control of Cuba, Puerto Rico, Guam, and the Philippines. The United States had fought the war to free Cuba from Spanish control. But now, rather than being independent, Cuba and the other territories were in the hands of the United States.

U.S. forces charge up San Juan Hill in Cuba in July 1898.

The United States gained the Philippines at the end of the Spanish-American War, but the Philippine people soon rebelled against American rule. More than 125,000 American soldiers fought in the Philippine-American War, including those pictured above.

Some people in the Philippines were unhappy that the United States controlled their country. They started fighting against American control. McKinley sent thousands of American sailors and soldiers to the Philippines. The Philippine-American War lasted until 1902. It was a bloody conflict. About 5,000 Americans and 200,000 Filipinos had died in the war by the time the United States won.

By winning the Spanish-American War and taking over new territory, the United States became one of the most powerful nations in the world. Many people considered McKinley a great leader because he made the United States a world power.

After the Spanish-American War, McKinley took several steps to demonstrate the United States' position as a world power. Now that it had control of the Philippines and Guam, the United States became more interested in the politics of Asian countries. In

1898, McKinley issued what was called an "Open Door" trade **policy** with China. Under an Open Door Policy, all nations have an equal right to trade with other nations. The United States could buy goods from China as well as sell American goods in China.

The Open Door Policy was announced in early 1900. A group of Chinese people called the Boxers were angry about it. Foreign nations controlled some Chinese ports. The Boxers wanted the foreigners to leave. They wanted to rid China of all foreign influence. To show that the United States supported an Open Door Policy, McKinley sent 5,000 U.S. soldiers to China to help Great Britain, Japan, Germany, Russia, and other countries end the war that was called the Boxer **Rebellion.** These countries were successful in stopping the rebellion, and the Open Door Policy with China remained in effect until the 1920s.

William McKinley traveled more than any other president before him.

Chinese Boxer troops walk through the streets of Tianjin, China. The city, which served as a base for many foreign businesses, was at the center of the Boxer Rebellion.

TEDDY ROOSEVELT AND THE ROUGH RIDERS

The Rough Riders were a group of American soldiers in the Spanish-American War who were led by Theodore "Teddy" Roosevelt (standing in center). Prior to the war, Roosevelt had served as an assistant secretary of the navy. He sometimes spoke out about the need for the United States to help Cuba. When it became clear that the United States would be involved in a war, Roosevelt quit his job and, along with army surgeon Leonard Wood, formed the First United States Volunteer Cavalry. The troop soon became known as the Rough Riders because it was made up of many cowboys, hunters, and outdoorsmen from the western United States. Large numbers of Native Americans and African Americans also joined the troop. The Rough Riders trained for only one month before they were sent into battle. They helped the United States gain control of Cuba. In 1899, Roosevelt published a book called *Rough Riders,* which included his personal story about his adventures in battle.

THE FINAL YEARS

In 1989, McKinley was ending his first four-year term as president. He had been successful in leading the country through difficult times with other countries. He had brought the United States to a position of being a world power. He was popular with the American people.

As the 1900 election approached, McKinley was again selected as the Republican candidate for president. The only question about McKinley's campaign was who would be the candidate for vice president. Garret Hobart, who had served as McKinley's vice president during his first term, had died in 1899. McKinley needed to find a new running mate. He and the Republicans chose Theodore Roosevelt, who by then was the governor of New York.

Theodore Roosevelt was McKinley's second vice president.

William McKinley was the first president to ride in an automobile.

McKinley and his wife loved flowers. After he was elected president, the rooms of the White House were always decorated with fresh flowers.

As in 1896, McKinley's opponent in the election was William Jennings Bryan. During the campaign, Bryan attacked McKinley on the issue of American **imperialism,** which means that he thought the United States government had too much control over other countries. Bryan was against U.S. control of the Philippines, Puerto Rico, and other places. He also said that McKinley had allowed large businesses to grow too powerful.

McKinley did not campaign during the election, yet he easily defeated Bryan. He began his second term as president of the United States in March 1901. In his second term, McKinley planned to spend more time dealing with **domestic** problems rather than **foreign policy.** He had hoped to address the problems of child labor, the poor treatment of workers, and the abuse of African Americans. But McKinley never had a chance to make a difference in these areas.

In 1901, Buffalo, New York, was hosting a major event called the Pan-American Exposition. The exposition was celebrating 100 years of progress in North and South America. On September 5, McKinley gave a speech at the Pan-American Exposition about America's role in the world. It was well received by both Americans and people from other countries.

The next day, September 6, McKinley appeared at the exposition again. This time, he was greeting visitors at a public reception. One of the people waiting in line to shake hands with the president was Leon Czolgosz (CHOLL-gosh). But Czolgosz did not shake

McKinley's hand. Instead, he shot the president twice. One bullet bounced off a button on McKinley's chest, but the other bullet went through his stomach, colon, and kidney and lodged in the muscles of his back. McKinley was rushed to the hospital. Surgeons operated immediately, but they could not find the bullet. In fact, they did not realize that the bullet had damaged any organs other than the stomach. They repaired the stomach and hoped that the president would make a full recovery.

Leon Czolgosz shot William McKinley on the afternoon of September 6, 1901. The president died eight days later.

THE MAN WHO
ASSASSINATED MCKINLEY

"I did my duty." Those were the words of Leon Czolgosz after he shot President McKinley. Czolgosz was 28 years old and living in Cleveland, Ohio, in 1901. He traveled to the Pan-American Exposition three days before he shot the president. In his confession to the police, he described his plans to shoot McKinley. He told police how he hid his gun with a handkerchief and described how he shot the president. Police said that Czolgosz seemed proud of what he had done.

Czolgosz did not have many friends and spent much of his free time reading newspapers and books. Over time, he came to hate the American system of government. He believed that all government officials were against working people. He thought that the president was "an enemy of the people" and that it was acceptable to kill him. Czolgosz shot McKinley on September 6, 1901. President McKinley died from the wounds on September 14. Czolgosz was quickly found guilty of the murder, and he was put to death on October 29, 1901.

McKinley seemed to be recovering in the days after the shooting. Everyone was confident that the president would soon be back to work. But on September 14, eight days after the shooting, the president died from an infection caused by the bullet. Theodore Roosevelt then became the 26th president.

The nation was in shock. Citizens of foreign countries were stunned because the world had lost a great leader. People forgot their political differences as they mourned the loss of President McKinley.

Ida McKinley was devastated by her husband's death. She missed him greatly and some said she visited McKinley's grave almost every day. Ida lived with her younger sister until her death in 1907.

Thousands of people crowded the streets of New York City for President McKinley's funeral procession. McKinley's body was brought from Buffalo to Washington, D.C., for his funeral, and then back to Ohio to be buried.

THE MCKINLEY MEMORIAL

The McKinley Memorial is located in Canton, Ohio, the city where McKinley lived. McKinley is buried at the monument, which was built between 1905 and 1907. Nearby is the William McKinley Presidential Library and Museum. Several exhibits allow visitors to experience life as it was in the late 1800s. In the McKinley Gallery, visitors can see a large collection of items from McKinley's life. In the Historical Hall, furnished rooms show how families lived between 1800 and 1900. The Industrial Hall highlights the different businesses that made the Canton, Ohio, area successful in the 1800s. The Street of Shops is a life-size model of an old town.

Today, people who study the presidents believe that William McKinley began to change the way a president worked. He communicated with the American people in new ways. He sent mailings and printed brochures to share information and spread his ideas through the newspapers. He found ways to promote his ideas so the American people had a good understanding of what was happening. He traveled all over the nation visiting with people, attending ceremonies, and making speeches.

William McKinley is credited with helping the United States become a world power. As a husband, he is remembered for his deep devotion to his wife. As a citizen, he is remembered for his honesty and excellent character. As a president, he is remembered for his ability to understand and take action on the issues important to the people of the United States and for his role in making the United States one of the world's most powerful nations.

The McKinley Memorial in Canton, Ohio, is located on a site McKinley had visited many times in his life. In fact, McKinley once suggested that it would make an excellent site for a monument to honor soldiers.

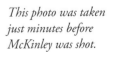

This photo was taken just minutes before McKinley was shot.

1840	1850	1860		1870

1843
William McKinley is born on January 29 in Niles, Ohio. He is the seventh of nine children. His parents are William and Nancy McKinley.

1852
McKinley's family moves to Poland, Ohio, so the children can get a better education. McKinley becomes a leading student at the Poland Academy, excelling in debate.

1860
McKinley enters Allegheny College in Meadville, Pennsylvania, but falls ill and returns home before the end of the school year.

1861
McKinley teaches and works in the post office in order to earn money to return to college. In April, the Civil War begins. McKinley joins the Union army.

1865
McKinley leaves the army and returns home to Ohio. He begins to study law, first with Judge Charles Glidden and then at the Albany Law School.

1867
McKinley settles in Canton, Ohio, and begins practicing law.

1869
McKinley is elected to his first public office, prosecuting attorney of Stark County, Ohio. He meets Ida Saxton, the daughter of a wealthy Canton banker.

1871
William McKinley and Ida Saxton marry in January. Their daughter, Katherine, is born on Christmas Day.

1873
The McKinleys' second daughter, Ida, is born, but lives only four and a half months.

1875
Katherine dies at the age of four.

1876
McKinley is elected to the U.S. House of Representatives. He serves until 1891.

1890

McKinley proposes the McKinley Tariff, which protects American businesses from foreign competition.

1891

McKinley is elected governor of Ohio. As governor, he proposes laws to help railroad workers and to deal with the problem of child labor. He helps solve problems between workers and business owners. While governor, he meets Mark Hanna, who will be an important supporter in his campaign for the presidency.

1896

The Republican Party selects McKinley as its presidential candidate. Mark Hanna raises more than $3.5 million for the campaign. McKinley is elected president of the United States. Garret Hobart is his vice president.

1897

McKinley is inaugurated on March 4.

1898

The battleship USS *Maine* mysteriously explodes in Havana, Cuba. More than 270 crewmembers are killed in the explosion. Americans blame Spain for the attack and encourage McKinley to declare war. The United States declares war on Spain. The Spanish-American War begins on April 25 and ends about 100 days later. After the war, the United States takes control of Cuba, Puerto Rico, Guam, and the Philippines. McKinley establishes the Open Door trade policy with China.

1899

Vice President Garret Hobart dies.

1900

Some Chinese people, upset with foreign influence in their country, start the Boxer Rebellion. McKinley is reelected president of the United States. Theodore Roosevelt is elected vice president.

1901

McKinley begins his second term as president. On September 6, he is shot twice by Leon Czolgosz at the Pan-American Exposition in Buffalo, New York. He dies on September 14. Vice President Theodore Roosevelt becomes the 26th president.

1907

Ida Saxton McKinley dies. The McKinley Memorial in Canton, Ohio, is dedicated.

1911

Congress creates the National McKinley Birthplace Memorial Association, which builds a memorial to the president in Niles, Ohio.

GLOSSARY

blockade (blah-KAYD) A blockade is a military tactic that keeps people and supplies from moving in or out of an area. U.S. ships formed a blockade in Cuba to trap Spanish ships during the Spanish-American War.

brevet (bruh-VET) A brevet is a certificate giving a military officer a temporarily higher rank. McKinley was a brevet major during the Civil War.

campaigns (kam-PAYNZ) A campaign is the process of running for an election, including activities such as giving speeches or attending rallies. McKinley ran his first presidential campaign from his home in Ohio.

candidate (KAN-duh-dayt) A candidate is a person running in an election. The Republicans chose McKinley as their candidate for president in both 1896 and 1900.

cavalry (KAV-ul-ree) A cavalry is an army unit that fights on horseback. Teddy Roosevelt's Rough Riders were a cavalry unit.

civil war (SIV-il WAR) A civil war is a war between opposing groups of citizens within the same country. The American Civil War began after the South left the Union.

Confederacy (kun-FED-ur-uh-see) The Confederacy is the states that left the Union in 1861. The Union defeated the Confederacy in the Civil War.

debating (dih-BAYT-ing) Debating is taking part in a contest in which opponents argue on opposite sides of an issue. While at the Poland Academy, McKinley was active in debating clubs.

disciplined (DIS-uh-plind) If a person is disciplined, he or she has good self-control. McKinley was disciplined.

domestic (duh-MES-tik) Domestic means having to do with one's own country rather than a foreign country. McKinley planned to pay more attention to domestic problems during his second term.

epilepsy (EP-uh-lep-see) Epilepsy is a disorder of the brain that sometimes causes seizures. Ida McKinley had epilepsy.

export (EKS-port) If you export an item, you send it to another country to be used or sold. In the 19th century, the United States did not export as many goods as it does today.

foreign policy (FOR-un PAWL-uh-see) A nation's foreign policy is how a country deals with other countries. McKinley was actively involved in U.S. foreign policy.

imperialism (im-PEER-ee-ul-iz-im) If a nation supports imperialism, it wants to rule or have authority over other countries. William Jennings Bryan was against imperialism.

imported (im-POR-ted) If goods are imported, they are brought in from another country to be sold. The McKinley Tariff placed a tax on imported goods.

inauguration (ih-naw-gyuh-RAY-shun) An inauguration is the ceremony that takes place when a new president begins a term. McKinley's first inauguration took place on March 4, 1897.

infantry (IN-fun-tree) An infantry is a group of soldiers trained and armed to fight on foot. McKinley joined the 23rd Ohio Volunteer Infantry.

mentor (MEN-tor) A mentor is a trusted adviser or teacher. Rutherford B. Hayes was McKinley's mentor.

negotiate (ne-GOH-she-ayt) If people negotiate, they talk things over and try to come to an agreement. McKinley encouraged Spain to negotiate with Cuba.

policy (PAWL-uh-see) A policy is a plan made to help run a government or other organization. The Chinese Boxers were against McKinley's Open Door Policy.

politics (PAWL-uh-tiks) Politics refers to the actions and practices of the government. McKinley became interested in politics during the Civil War.

prosperity (prah-SPAYR-uh-tee) Prosperity is success or economic well-being. In the 1896 presidential campaign, McKinley promised to bring the nation prosperity.

rebellion (rih-BEL-yen) A rebellion is a fight against one's government. A group of Chinese people started the Boxer Rebellion to push foreign countries out of China.

revolution (rev-uh-LOO-shun) A revolution is something that causes a complete change in government. The American Revolution was a war fought between the United States and Great Britain.

seizures (SEE-zhurz) Seizures are sudden attacks in which a person often faints or moves uncontrollably. Ida McKinley suffered from seizures.

territories (TAYR-uh-tor-eez) Territories are large areas of land, especially land that belongs to a government. Northerners did not want slavery to expand into the new U.S. territories.

treaty (TREE-tee) A treaty is a formal agreement made between nations. The Treaty of Paris ended the Spanish-American War.

Union (YOON-yen) A union is the joining together of two people or groups of people, such as states. During the Civil War, the Union fought the Confederacy.

THE UNITED STATES GOVERNMENT

T he United States government is divided into three equal branches: the executive, the legislative, and the judicial. This division helps prevent abuses of power because each branch has to answer to the other two. No one branch can become too powerful.

EXECUTIVE BRANCH

PRESIDENT
VICE PRESIDENT
DEPARTMENTS

The job of the executive branch is to enforce the laws. It is headed by the president, who serves as the spokesperson for the United States around the world. The president signs bills into law and appoints important officials such as federal judges. He or she is also the commander in chief of the U.S. military. The president is assisted by the vice president, who takes over if the president dies or cannot carry out the duties of the office.

The executive branch also includes various departments, each focused on a specific topic. They include the Defense Department, the Justice Department, and the Agriculture Department. The department heads, along with other officials such as the vice president, serve as the president's closest advisers, called the cabinet.

LEGISLATIVE BRANCH

CONGRESS
Senate and
House of Representatives

The job of the legislative branch is to make the laws. It consists of Congress, which is divided into two parts: the Senate and the House of Representatives. The Senate has 100 members, and the House of Representatives has 435 members. Each state has two senators. The number of representatives a state has varies depending on the state's population.

Besides making laws, Congress also passes budgets and enacts taxes. In addition, it is responsible for declaring war, maintaining the military, and regulating trade with other countries.

JUDICIAL BRANCH

SUPREME COURT
COURTS OF APPEALS
DISTRICT COURTS

The job of the judicial branch is to interpret the laws. It consists of the nation's federal courts. Trials are held in district courts. During trials, judges must decide what laws mean and how they apply. Courts of appeals review the decisions made in district courts.

The nation's highest court is the Supreme Court. If someone disagrees with a court of appeals ruling, he or she can ask the Supreme Court to review it. The Supreme Court may refuse. The Supreme Court makes sure that decisions and laws do not violate the Constitution.

CHOOSING
THE PRESIDENT

It may seem odd, but American voters don't elect the president directly. Instead, the president is chosen using what is called the Electoral College.

Each state gets as many votes in the Electoral College as its combined total of senators and representatives in Congress. For example, Iowa has two senators and five representatives, so it gets seven electoral votes. Although the District of Columbia does not have any voting members in Congress, it gets three electoral votes. Usually, the candidate who wins the most votes in any given state receives all of that state's electoral votes.

To become president, a candidate must get more than half of the Electoral College votes. There are a total of 538 votes in the Electoral College, so a candidate needs 270 votes to win. If nobody receives 270 Electoral College votes, the House of Representatives chooses the president.

With the Electoral College system, the person who receives the most votes nationwide does not always receive the most electoral votes. This happened most recently in 2000, when Al Gore received half a million more national votes than George W. Bush. Bush became president because he had more Electoral College votes.

THE WHITE HOUSE

The White House is the official home of the president of the United States. It is located at 1600 Pennsylvania Avenue NW in Washington, D.C. In 1792, a contest was held to select the architect who would design the president's home. James Hoban won. Construction took eight years.

The first president, George Washington, never lived in the White House. The second president, John Adams, moved into the house in 1800, though the inside was not yet complete. During the War of 1812, British soldiers burned down much of the White House. It was rebuilt several years later.

The White House was changed through the years. Porches were added, and President Theodore Roosevelt added the West Wing. President William Taft changed the shape of the presidential office, making it into the famous Oval Office. While Harry Truman was president, the old house was discovered to be structurally weak. All the walls were reinforced with steel, and the rooms were rebuilt.

Today, the White House has 132 rooms (including 35 bathrooms), 28 fireplaces, and 3 elevators. It takes 570 gallons of paint to cover the outside of the six-story building. The White House provides the president with many ways to relax. It includes a putting green, a jogging track, a swimming pool, a tennis court, and beautifully landscaped gardens. The White House also has a movie theater, a billiard room, and a one-lane bowling alley.

PRESIDENTIAL PERKS

The job of president of the United States is challenging. It is probably one of the most stressful jobs in the world. Because of this, presidents are paid well, though not nearly as well as the leaders of large corporations. In 2007, the president earned $400,000 a year. Presidents also receive extra benefits that make the demanding job a little more appealing.

★ **Camp David:** In the 1940s, President Franklin D. Roosevelt chose this heavily wooded spot in the mountains of Maryland to be the presidential retreat, where presidents can relax. Even though it is a retreat, world business is conducted there. Most famously, President Jimmy Carter met with Middle Eastern leaders at Camp David in 1978. The result was a peace agreement between Israel and Egypt.

★ *Air Force One:* The president flies on a jet called *Air Force One.* It is a Boeing 747-200B that has been modified to meet the president's needs.

Air Force One is the size of a large home. It is equipped with a dining room, sleeping quarters, a conference room, and office space. It also has two kitchens that can provide food for up to 50 people.

★ **The Secret Service:** While not the most glamorous of the president's perks, the Secret Service is one of the most important. The Secret Service is a group of highly trained agents who protect the president and the president's family.

★ **The Presidential State Car:** The presidential limousine is a stretch Cadillac DTS.

It has been armored to protect the president in case of attack. Inside the plush car are a foldaway desk, an entertainment center, and a communications console.

★ **The Food:** The White House has five chefs who will make any food the president wants. The White House also has an extensive wine collection.

★ **Retirement:** A former president receives a pension, or retirement pay, of just under $180,000 a year. Former presidents also receive Secret Service protection for the rest of their lives.

FACTS

QUALIFICATIONS

To run for president, a candidate must

* be at least 35 years old
* be a citizen who was born in the United States
* have lived in the United States for 14 years

TERM OF OFFICE

A president's term of office is four years.
No president can stay in office for more than two terms.

ELECTION DATE

The presidential election takes place every four years on the first Tuesday of November.

INAUGURATION DATE

Presidents are inaugurated on January 20.

OATH OF OFFICE

I do solemnly swear I will faithfully execute the office of the President of the United States and will to the best of my ability preserve, protect, and defend the Constitution of the United States.

WRITE A LETTER TO THE PRESIDENT

One of the best things about being a U.S. citizen is that Americans get to participate in their government. They can speak out if they feel government leaders aren't doing their jobs. They can also praise leaders who are going the extra mile. Do you have something you'd like the president to do? Should the president worry more about the environment and encourage people to recycle? Should the government spend more money on our schools? You can write a letter to the president to say how you feel!

1600 Pennsylvania Avenue
Washington, D.C. 20500
You can even send an e-mail to: president@whitehouse.gov

BOOKS

Doak, Robin. *William McKinley*. Minneapolis: Compass Point Books, 2004.

Edge, Laura B. *William McKinley*. Minneapolis: Twenty-First Century Books, 2007.

Langellier, John P. *Uncle Sam's Little Wars: The Spanish-American War, Philippine Insurrection, and Boxer Rebellion*. Philadelphia: Chelsea House, 2002.

Riehecky, Janet. *William McKinley: America's 25th President*. New York: Children's Press, 2004.

Santella, Andrew. *Roosevelt's Rough Riders*. Minneapolis: Compass Point Books, 2006.

VIDEOS

The History Channel Presents The Presidents. DVD (New York: A&E Home Video, 2005).

National Geographic's Inside the White House. DVD (Washington, DC: National Geographic Video, 2003).

INTERNET SITES

Visit our Web page for lots of links about William McKinley and other U.S. presidents:

http://www.childsworld.com/links

Note to Parents, Teachers, and Librarians: We routinely verify our Web links to make sure they are safe, active sites—so encourage your readers to check them out!

INDEX